# WHAT IF A SHARK HAD A PARTY?

Aleksei Bitskoff &
Camilla de la Bédoyère

QEB

# A great white shark

Imagine a great white shark came to stay. What do you think would happen?

is a huge, meat-eating fish.
Discover fascinating facts about how he lives, what he eats, and how big he really is!

# What if a shark went to a water park?

It would be his idea of a great day out!

Sharks are just the right shape for speeding through water . . .

He'd like the pool best. Sharks are fish, so they have **gills** for breathing underwater.
. . . or zoooming down slides!

What if a shark went to the dentist?

He would be there a long time.

He wouldn't need a filling. Sharks lose teeth all the time but they keep growing new ones.

# How would a shark get to school?

He is far too big to squeeze inside a car, so you could strap him to the roof!

Great white sharks can grow up to 20 feet long, but most are about 15 feet. That's the length of a family car!
The biggest great white shark ever found was 23 feet long!

What if a shark had a party?
He would have a
barbecue because sharks
looooooove
to eat meat!

He wouldn't need to eat again for two weeks!

# Could a shark do gymnastics?

Sharks have strong and bendy bodies that are perfect for gymnastics.

Shark skeletons are made from **cartilage**, which is lighter and more flexible than bone.

He could leap high over a bar. Great white sharks jump right out of the water to catch seals, sea lions, and seabirds.

Their awesome leaps can reach more than 8 feet.

That's higher than any human has ever jumped!

# Could a shark play tennis?

A shark would be great at ball games.
He could use his big fins or powerful tail to hit a ball.

Sharks also have super senses.
They know when fish are swimming behind or below them, and can even sense their heartbeats!

# What if a shark needs to go pee?

He could find the toilet with his eyes shut just by following his nose.

Sharks have an amazing sense of smell. They could smell a teaspoon of pee in a whole swimming pool!

# Could a shark play on a seesaw?

He would need a big seesaw, and lots of children to help balance him.

A fully grown great white shark weighs about

4,500 pounds.

By contrast, this dwarf lantern shark is the smallest known shark. It only weighs 0.5 ounces!

# Would a shark like to play in the snow?

He would love it!

Great white sharks don't mind getting chilly because they live in cool oceans.

Whooshing downhill on a sled would be just as much fun as speeding through the ocean.
The shortfin mako is the fastest of all sharks, speeding through the ocean at around 42 miles per hour!

# Could a shark join a choir?

He could conduct a choir, but he couldn't sing in one.

Sharks don't have voices, and they swim in total silence.

Their skin is covered with special scales that help them slip soundlessly through the water ...
so no one can
hear
them
coming!
Shark skin is covered with scales that are coated with **enamel**. These scales are called **denticles**, and they help water to move smoothly over a shark.

# What would a shark do at bedtime?

Sharks never get sleepy, so he would keep everyone else awake!

When sharks breathe, water flows between their **gill slits**. They absorb oxygen from the water as it passes through.
Great white sharks can only breathe when they are swimming, so they need to keep moving all the time.

# The Parts of a Shark

**Gill slits**
Most sharks have five on each side of their body.

**Large eyes**
Sharks have no eyelids.

**Powerful jaws**
These are packed with rows of teeth.

**Pectoral fin**
Fish, dolphins, and whales have these on either side of their body.

First dorsal fin
Some sharks have spines on their dorsal fins too.
Second dorsal fin
This is usually smaller than the first.
Tail fin
This fin shape is common in fast-swimming sharks.
Anal fin
Not all sharks have anal fins.

# SHARK GALLERY

HELP!

### Thresher Shark
Killer skill: Whacking
Typical length: 102-197"
Habitat: Coast and open ocean

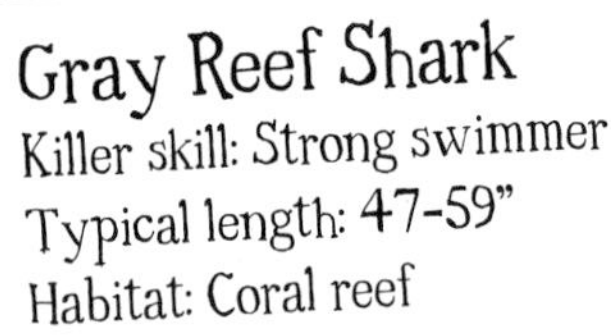

### Gray Reef Shark
Killer skill: Strong swimmer
Typical length: 47-59"
Habitat: Coral reef

### Spiny Dogfish
Killer skill: Long-lived
Typical length: 20-39"
Habitat: Coastal

### Shortfin Mako
Killer skill: Speed
Typical length: 79-118"
Habitat: Coast and open ocean

### Port Jackson Shark
Killer skill: Hiding
Typical length: 28-39"
Habitat: Sandy sea bed

### Dwarf Lantern Shark
Killer skill: Light-maker
Typical length: 6.3-8"
Habitat: Continental slope

**Lemon Shark**
Killer skill: Stocky and strong
Typical length: 87-95"
Habitat: Coastal

**Great White Shark**
Killer skill: Big
Typical length: 138-197"
Habitat: Coast and open ocean

**Sand Tiger Shark**
Killer skill: Teeth
Typical length: 75-118"
Habitat: Warm coast

**Tiger shark**
Killer skill: Not picky
Typical length: 91-138"
Habitat: Continental shelf

This symbol means that these sharks are close to being endangered.

This symbol means that these sharks are already endangered—they may die out soon.

**Greenland Shark**
Killer skill: Copes with cold
Typical length: 118-236"
Habitat: Cold coast

**Angelshark**
Killer skill: Hiding
Typical length: 32-71"
Habitat: Seabed

**Basking Shark**
Killer skill: Size
Typical length: 157-315"
Habitat: Open ocean

**Whale Shark**
Killer skill: Super-size
Typical length: 236-591"
Habitat: Coast and open ocean

**Great Hammerhead**
Killer skill: Super senses
Typical length: 91-158"
Habitat: Coast and open ocean

Blue Shark
Killer skill: Super swimmer
Typical length: 71-87"
Habitat: Open ocean

Bramble Shark
Killer skill: Stealthy
Typical length: 147-87"
Habitat: Deep sea

Frilled Shark
Killer skill: Deep-sea survivor
Typical length: 35-51"
Habitat: Deep sea

Megamouth Shark
Killer skill: Size
Typical length: 167-217"
Habitat: Warm ocean

Porbeagle
Killer skill: Speed
Typical length: 63-98"
Habitat: Cold waters

Pyjama Shark
Killer skill: Night hunter
Typical length: 28-35"
Habitat: Sea bed

# Glossary

**cartilage**
a strong, flexible fiber in animals' bones. Shark skeletons are made from cartilage

**denticles**
toothlike scales on a shark's skin

**enamel**
a tough, glossy substance. This is the same material that makes our teeth hard

**gills**
organs inside the body of a fish used for breathing in water

**gill slits**
openings (slits or gaps) on a shark's body where water passes through

**prey**
an animal that is hunted and eaten by other animals

Publisher: Zeta Jones
Associate Publisher: Maxime Boucknooghe
Editorial Director: Victoria Garrard
Editor: Joanna McInerney
Art Director: Miranda Snow
Designer: Mike Henson



First published in the United States by
QEB Publishing, Inc.
6 Orchard
Lake Forest, CA 92630

www.qed-publishing.co.uk



A CIP record for this book is available from the Library of Congress.

ISBN 978 1 60992 984 8

Printed in China